AF332936

The Dragon Hammer

and

The Tale of Oniroku

Two Plays from the Far East
for Young People to Read and Perform

by Joanna Halpert Kraus

illustrated by Marisabina Russo

NEW PLAYS, INC., ROWAYTON, CONNECTICUT

ACKNOWLEDGEMENTS

I would like to express my gratitude to Samuel Im for his generous research assistance while adapting *The Dragon Hammer*.

Also, I would like to thank Timothy Yang Kun Kraus for his construction of a Korean kite and his help in creating the goblin noises.

The Dragon Hammer comes from an old fairy tale, "The Mallet of Wealth," from the town of Onyang in the southeast section of Korea. Zong, In-Sob, comp. trans. *Folk Tales from Korea.* (London: Routledge and Kegan Paul, Ltd., 1952).

The Tale of Oniroku comes from an old folk tale, "The Carpenter and Oniroku," from the prefecture of Iwate in the northeast section of Japan. A. Yanagida, Kunion, ed. *Nihon Mukashibanashi Meii* (Tokyo: Nippon Hoso Kyokai, 1948).

Library of Congress catalog card number: 77-828-57

The Dragon Hammer

Cast of Characters

Bang-Su, a poor boy who finds the magic hammer

Mother

Head Goblin

Two Other Goblins

Chang-Gil, a sly, selfish boy

Mountain Spirits, who play the Walnut Tree, the Mountain,
and display the Sun and Moon

Three Villagers

Settings

The play takes place by a walnut tree
high up in the mountains of Korea, and
near Bang-Su's home in a village nearby,
a long time ago, when people believed in
goblins and goblins believed in people.

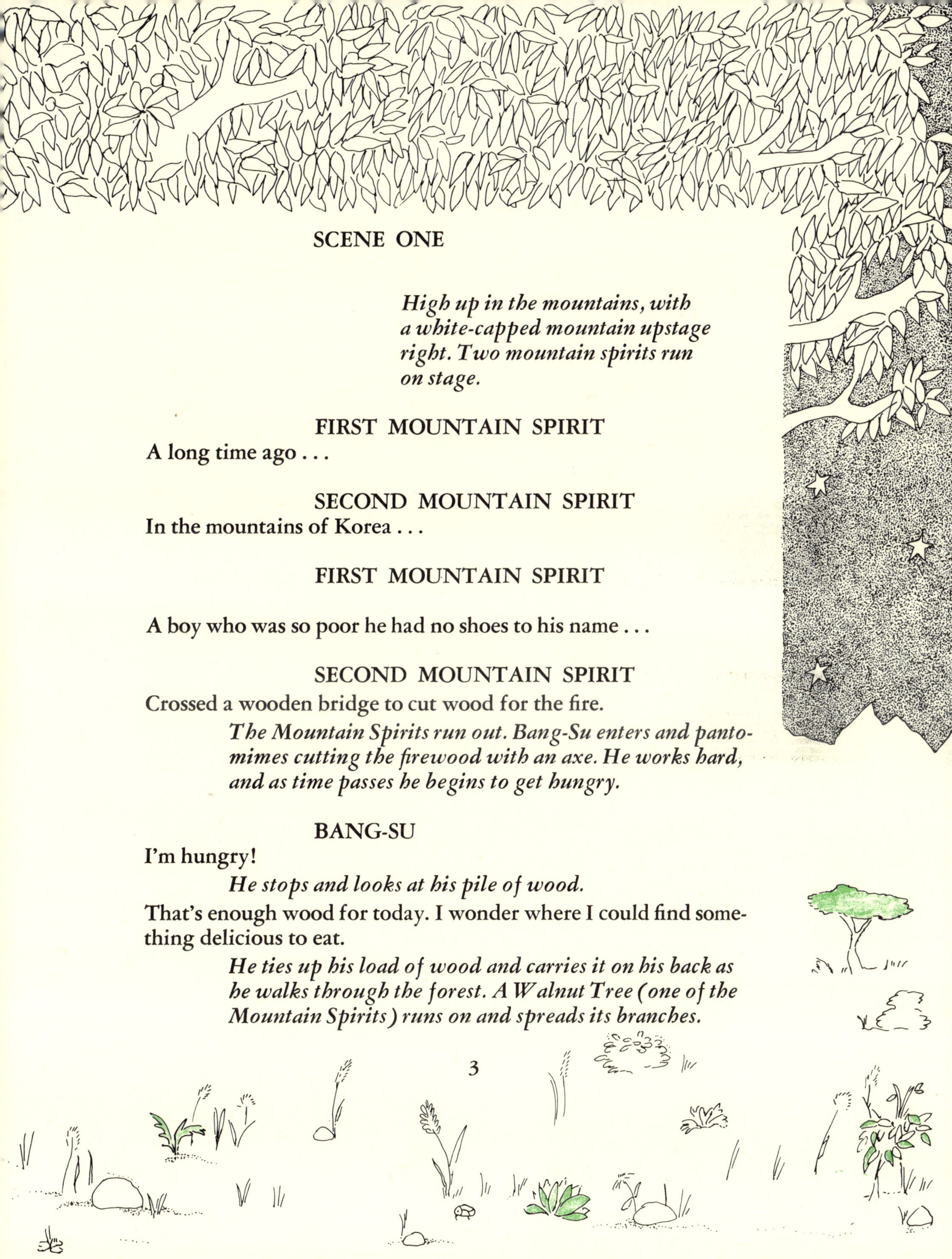

SCENE ONE

*High up in the mountains, with
a white-capped mountain upstage
right. Two mountain spirits run
on stage.*

FIRST MOUNTAIN SPIRIT

A long time ago . . .

SECOND MOUNTAIN SPIRIT

In the mountains of Korea . . .

FIRST MOUNTAIN SPIRIT

A boy who was so poor he had no shoes to his name . . .

SECOND MOUNTAIN SPIRIT

Crossed a wooden bridge to cut wood for the fire.

*The Mountain Spirits run out. Bang-Su enters and panto-
mimes cutting the firewood with an axe. He works hard,
and as time passes he begins to get hungry.*

BANG-SU

I'm hungry!

He stops and looks at his pile of wood.

That's enough wood for today. I wonder where I could find something delicious to eat.

*He ties up his load of wood and carries it on his back as
he walks through the forest. A Walnut Tree (one of the
Mountain Spirits) runs on and spreads its branches.*

3

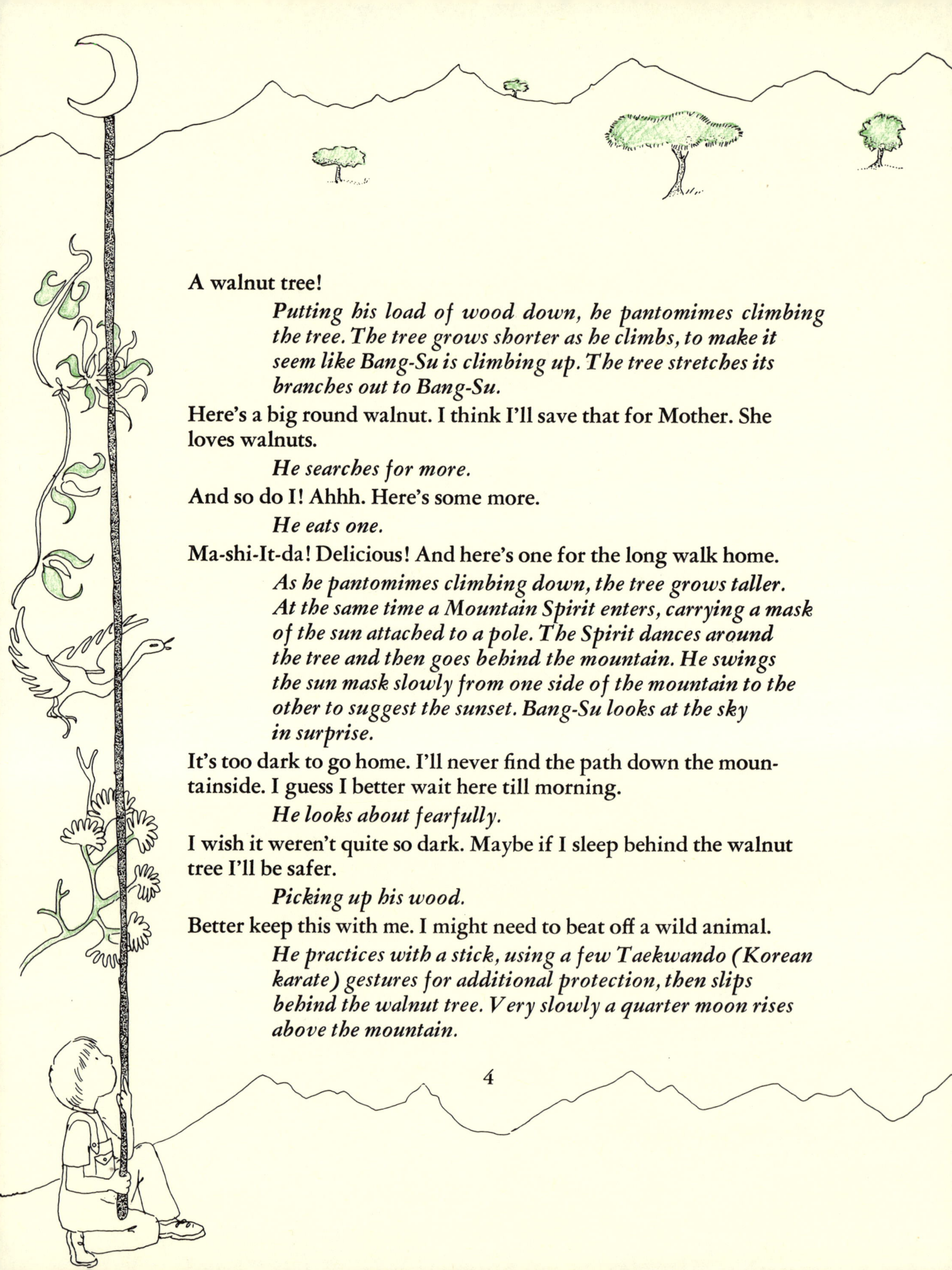

A walnut tree!

> *Putting his load of wood down, he pantomimes climbing
> the tree. The tree grows shorter as he climbs, to make it
> seem like Bang-Su is climbing up. The tree stretches its
> branches out to Bang-Su.*

Here's a big round walnut. I think I'll save that for Mother. She
loves walnuts.

> *He searches for more.*

And so do I! Ahhh. Here's some more.

> *He eats one.*

Ma-shi-It-da! Delicious! And here's one for the long walk home.

> *As he pantomimes climbing down, the tree grows taller.
> At the same time a Mountain Spirit enters, carrying a mask
> of the sun attached to a pole. The Spirit dances around
> the tree and then goes behind the mountain. He swings
> the sun mask slowly from one side of the mountain to the
> other to suggest the sunset. Bang-Su looks at the sky
> in surprise.*

It's too dark to go home. I'll never find the path down the moun-
tainside. I guess I better wait here till morning.

> *He looks about fearfully.*

I wish it weren't quite so dark. Maybe if I sleep behind the walnut
tree I'll be safer.

> *Picking up his wood.*

Better keep this with me. I might need to beat off a wild animal.

> *He practices with a stick, using a few Taekwando (Korean
> karate) gestures for additional protection, then slips
> behind the walnut tree. Very slowly a quarter moon rises
> above the mountain.*

4

In through the dark forest the Goblins creep, leap, and jump from all sides. When they find each other they somersault and jump about, making a goblin-like commotion as they greet each other excitedly.

HEAD GOBLIN
Tchakata . . . tchakata . . . tchakat . . . tchakat.

FIRST GOBLIN
Ka . . . ka . . . ka . . . ka . . , Ka . . . ka . . . ka . . . ka.

SECOND GOBLIN
Jiggee . . . Giggee . . . giggee . . . Jigee . . . Jiggee . . . Jiggee.

HEAD GOBLIN
with a somersault

FIRST GOBLIN
Ba . . . Ba . . . Ba . . . Ba . . . Ba . . . Ba . . . Ba . . . Ba . . . Ba . . .

SECOND GOBLIN
squeaking like a door
Eh . . . Eh . . . Eh . . . Eh . . . Eh . . . Eh . . . Eh . . . Eh . . . Eh . . .

ALL THREE GOBLINS
in solemn low voices
OH, UMMMMMM. OH, UMMMMMM. UH, UMMMMMM

HEAD GOBLIN
And now for our New Year's Feast.

FIRST GOBLIN
Bring out the goblin hammer.

SECOND GOBLIN
The hammer no mortal has ever found.

FIRST GOBLIN
The hammer no human can lift from the ground.
> *The Head Goblin takes the dragon hammer from his belt,
> and, with all his goblin strength, swings, bends, and
> pounds the earth, chanting.*

HEAD GOBLIN
Tudurag-tag-tag.

FIRST AND SECOND GOBLINS
Tudurag-tag-tag.

HEAD GOBLIN
Rice appear.
> *The Goblins crowd around a large rice dish that suddenly
> appears, and it is evident from the loud smacks and
> chewing sounds that they are all hungry.*

FIRST GOBLIN
Let's have New Year's wine.

SECOND GOBLIN
And rice-cake soup. That's the best part of the New Year's feast!

FIRST GOBLIN
I like meat.

SECOND GOBLIN

And fruit.

HEAD GOBLIN

Ready, Goblins?

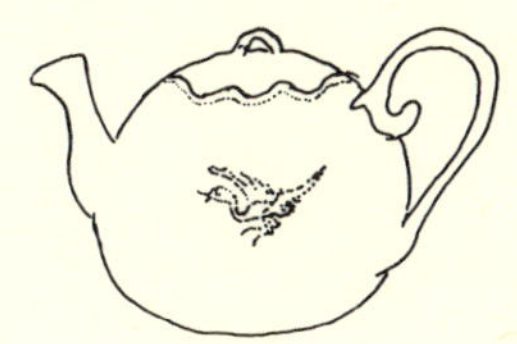

> *The goblins make a circle. Again the Head Goblin lifts the hammer and swings with all his might down to the earth, chanting.*

Tudurag-tag-tag.

FIRST AND SECOND GOBLINS

Tudurag-tag-tag.

HEAD GOBLIN

New Year's wine.

FIRST AND SECOND GOBLINS

New Year's wine.

HEAD GOBLIN

Rice-cake soup.

FIRST AND SECOND GOBLINS

Rice-cake soup.

HEAD GOBLIN

Meat and fruit.

FIRST AND SECOND GOBLINS

Meat and fruit!

> *With loud exclamations, the Goblins pantomime the appearance of this marvelous feast. They sit on the ground and eat, using chopsticks and spoons.*

HEAD GOBLIN

UMMMMM.

FIRST AND SECOND GOBLINS

Slurp! Slurp.

> *The Head Goblin pours warm wine from a teapot. Each of the Goblins holds a bowl of wine in one hand and drinks happily from it.*

HEAD GOBLIN

My friends, once there was goblin writing on the handle of this hammer. Years ago it glittered in the moonlight. Now it has been worn away by time.

FIRST GOBLIN

I remember! I remember! It was a warning to all humans.

> *"If ever I be found*
> *I will not lift from the ground."*

Pass the rice-cake soup, please.

HEAD GOBLIN

> *Passing the bowl of soup*

But there was more written long ago on the other side of the hammer.

FIRST GOBLIN

> *Continuing to feast*

Tell us what it said. Ummm . . . this year's rice-cake soup is the best we've ever had.

HEAD GOBLIN

It was many, many bowls of rice-cake soup ago . . .

> *Touching the dragon hammer*

Perhaps I can still remember . . .

8

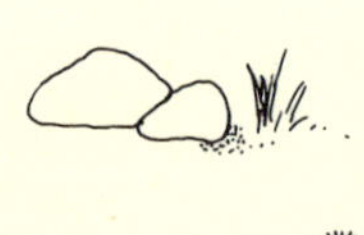

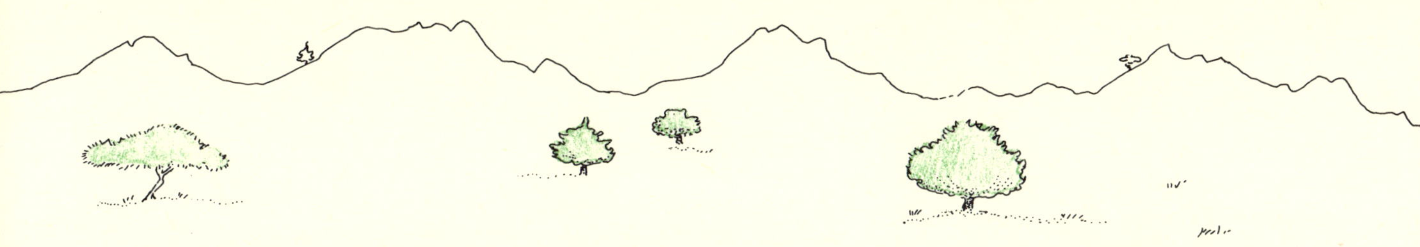

He thinks as he holds the hammer
Ahhh, yes.

> *"But one who is kind to family and friend*
> *Will find me freely in the end."*

FIRST GOBLIN
Sipping the wine
But the hammer is safe with us. It has been for centuries. Any mortal
who is selfish . . . or greedy . . . or lazy . . . can never, NEVER lift
the hammer.

FIRST GOBLIN
Once I saw a mortal find the hammer.

SECOND GOBLIN
What happened?

HEAD GOBLIN
My friends, it was long ago. Tigers ran through the towns scaring
everyone. One cold night some village men went out to hunt
the tigers.

FIRST GOBLIN
I remember this story. One of them saw the dragon hammer's eyes.
He stopped. He forgot the tigers. He forgot his friends.
When they called for help, he did not hear them.

HEAD GOBLIN
Such greed is like a sickness, but there is no mountain plant
to cure it!

SECOND GOBLIN
What did he do?

FIRST GOBLIN

First he pushed, then he pulled, then he kicked. But the dragon hammer NEVER moved.

HEAD GOBLIN

Stretching and yawning

All this good food and New Year's wine . . .

> *yawn*

has made me

> *yawn*

t . . . i . . . r . . . e . . . d.

FIRST GOBLIN

Me too.

SECOND GOBLIN

Me too.

HEAD GOBLIN

Good night.

> *With sighs of contentment one by one the goblins fall asleep and the dragon hammer rolls out of the Head Goblin's hand onto the ground. There is silence for a few seconds.*

BANG-SU

Peers out in amazement

All that food! I'm so hungry.

> *Just then the Second Goblin stirs, waving his arms and muttering in his sleep. Bang-Su decides he'd better not risk taking any food.*

I better eat a walnut.
> *He takes a large one from his pocket and cracks it loudly.*

HEAD GOBLIN
> *Jumping up*

HELP! The earth is splitting. Run for your lives!
> *In his haste, he forgets the dragon hammer.*

FIRST GOBLIN
> *As the Goblins run off*

Run for your lives!

SECOND GOBLIN

Leave the forest!

BANG-SU
> *Creeping out from behind the tree, hungrily he
> eats a left-over rice-cake. Then in the moonlight
> he suddenly sees the dragon hammer.*

The dragon hammer!
> *Bends down to look at it*

No harm in just looking at it.
> *As he looks at it*

Oh, those dragon eyes look almost real.
> *He starts to touch the hammer with a finger, then backs
> away hastily. Thoughtfully he circles the hammer.*

Well, I could just *touch it*. That wouldn't hurt. And my mother
will never believe that I saw the dragon hammer if I don't describe
it exactly.
> *Puts his hand around the handle to measure it*

The handle is carved of wood and . . .

11

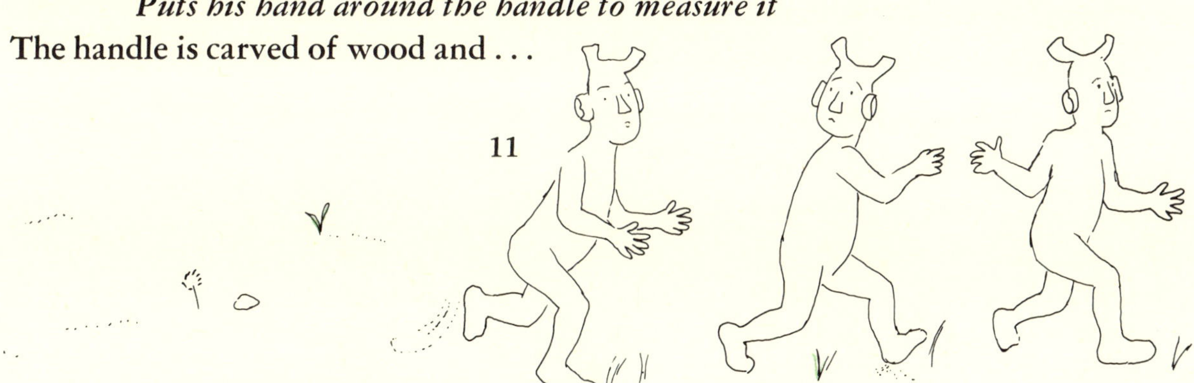

To his amazement, it lifts from the ground
It moved. The dragon hammer MOVED!
    He examines it in his hand reverently and cautiously
Will it work for *me???*
    Wondering
Could I get a black pony?
    He imagines himself galloping away, then stops.
But where would I keep it, when it snows?
    Gazing at the hammer he dreams
Of all the things I could wish for . . .
    Scarcely able to say it
What I want most . . . is a pair of . . . boots! Leather boots!
Splendid boots! Boots like the King's.
    He closes his eyes and dreams of the boots.
Boots! Beautiful boots!
    Swings, bends, and pounds the earth with the hammer,
    chanting
Tudurag-tag-tag. Tudurag-tag-tag. Boots appear.
    Instantly the boots appear at the foot of the walnut tree.
    Bang-Su turns around and sees them.
OOOhhhh!!
    He puts them on carefully, admiring them the whole time.
    The moon goes down.
They fit perfectly. Just my size.
    He puts the hammer in his belt and says happily
Now I'll run all the way home!
    Bang-Su runs out. The Tree runs off and the mountain
    disappears as the scene changes.

SCENE TWO

*Outside Bang-Su's home, a round mud
hut with a rice straw thatched roof.
Attached to the house is a traditional
Korean kite. Near the house is a large
earthenware jar, which holds a supply of
kimchi (spiced cabbage) for the winter.*

*Chang-Gil creeps on, looks to see if anyone is watching
him, then creeps in further. He steals up to the kite and
starts to unfasten it.*

CHANG-GIL

Now, I'll just take Bang-Su's kite to my house . . .

He sees Bang-Su coming and lets go of the kite in a hurry.

Too late! Here he comes.

He darts behind the storage jar.

BANG-SU

Mother! Mother!

*As she comes out, Bang-Su stands straight with hands at
his side and bows from the waist in respect, then continues.*

Look what I have! Look what I found.

He puts down his axe and wood.

MOTHER

Happily

Oh, Bang-Su, I'm glad to see you. Did you have to stay on the
mountain all night? I was so worried when I heard the wind howl.
I thought the bridge had come down.

She looks at the wood.

Oh, this is excellent firewood.

BANG-SU
Excitedly
Oh, but it's not the wood, Mother, I want you to see. Last night, on the mountains . . . by the moonlight . . . there were three goblins —and look!

MOTHER
Gasps, then says slowly
Bang Su—is it possible? Is it really the dragon hammer?
> *At these words Chang-Gil pokes his head out, then jumps back.*

Did you try it out? Maybe it's a joke or a trick. No one in our village has ever found it before.

BANG-SU
No, it's real, Mother. Look! Look at my leather boots.

MOTHER
Boots, Bang-Su?
> *She sees them for the first time and in surprise she examines them.*

And just the right size. Ah, these are goblin's boots. Look how carefully they are made. They will never wear out!
> *Realizing how important the hammer could be*

Can the hammer bring cooked rice for our breakfast?

BANG-SU
Watch!

> *Chang-Gil can't resist watching and half his head peers out from behind the jar. Bang-Su swings the hammer with all his might, bends and pounds the ground.*

Tudurag-tag-tag. Tudurag-tag-tag. Rice appear.

CHANG-GIL
Jumping up in his amazement
Look!

14

MOTHER
Not noticing Chang-Gil

So much rice! And cooked just the way we like it. Oh, Bang-Su, you have brought a great honor to our family.

Chang-Gil hides again.

Long ago it was said that only a person with a kind heart and a wise mind could ever lift the hammer from the ground.

Excitedly

Now, tell me all about it? Where were you when you saw the hammer? Did the goblins see you?

BANG-SU

I want to tell you all about it . . .

Smelling rice

But that rice smells so good. Let's eat breakfast first. I'm hungry! And I ran all the way home!

MOTHER
Warmly

Of course.

Bang-Su lifts the rice bowl up, leaving the hammer on the ground.

I'm hungry too. I was waiting for you to come.

They walk into the house. As soon as they are gone, Chang-Gil darts over to the hammer.

CHANG-GIL

"Kind heart!" I don't believe all that nonsense!

He tries to yank the hammer from the ground, but it won't budge. He struggles.

It's stuck! Never mind. There's another way.

He creeps to the doorway and eavesdrops.

First . . . climb the mountain . . .

Listening

Second, chop wood.

Listening

Third, find the walnut tree and hide behind it.

Listening

Then crack the walnut . . . and scare the goblins away! That's easy.
I'll even take Bang-Su's axe. I haven't used mine in so long, it's rusty.

Chang-Gil picks up the axe.

I'll bring it back tomorrow. *After* I find the dragon hammer I won't
need anybody's axe . . . ever again.

Happily

I'll never have to work. I'll just play—all day long!

*He goes out. The hut and the storage jar are carried
off as The Mountain reappears.*

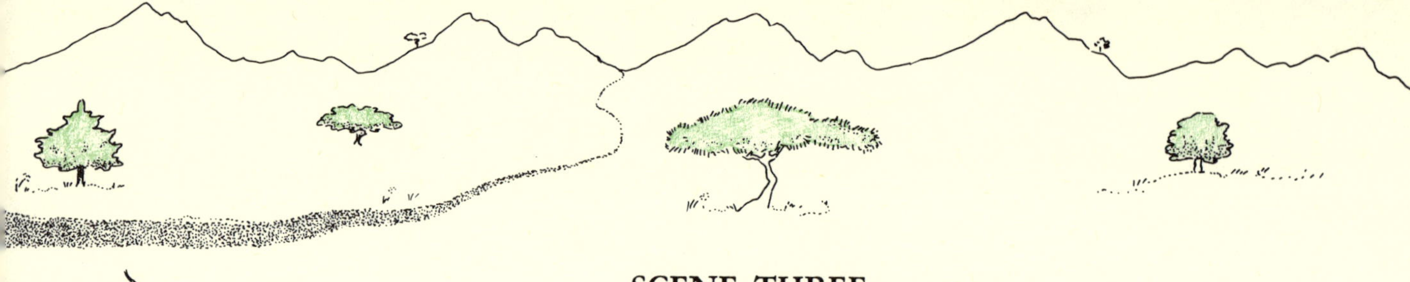

SCENE THREE

High up in the mountains
Chang-Gil enters panting.

CHANG-GIL

That was hard work. I never climbed the mountain before. And this axe is too heavy.

He flings it down.

Now to find that walnut tree.

He looks around and sees a piece of rice-cake on the ground.

Here's a piece of rice-cake. The goblin's tree can't be far.

The Walnut Tree comes on and spreads its branches.

That looks like a walnut tree.

He jumps up and snatches a nut.

It *is* the walnut tree.

He drags the axe over and hides behind the tree. Peeking out.

Now to get one of those dragon hammers for myself.

He hides again. A Mountain Spirit enters carrying the mask of the Sun attached to a pole, dances around the tree, and then goes behind the mountain. He swings the sun mask slowly from one side of the mountain to the other to suggest the sunset. Very slowly a quarter moon rises above the mountain. Soon there is a clattering commotion as the Goblins jump and leap in from all sides, making noises as before.

ALL THREE GOBLINS

As they somersault to the center

WHOOOOKKKKKK!!!

They form a circle and sit down. Immediately Chang-Gil loudly cracks a walnut.

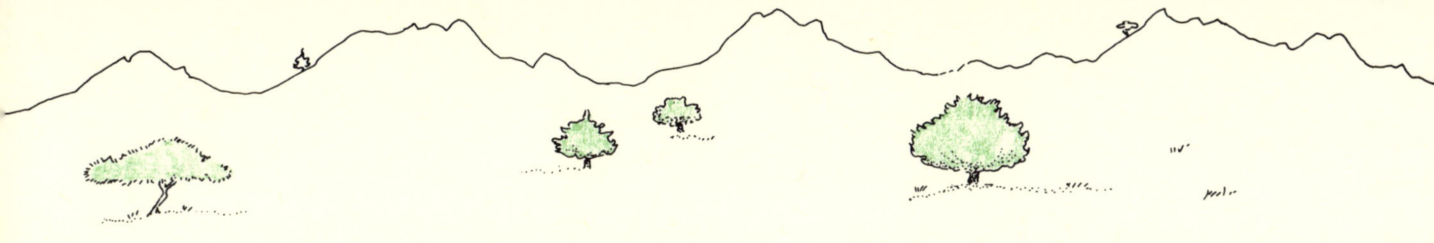

HEAD GOBLIN

Stop!

FIRST GOBLIN

A thief!

SECOND GOBLIN

Could it be the same person who found our ancient dragon hammer?

FIRST GOBLIN

Heatedly

Well, no creature is going to steal our *new* dragon hammer. It took
me all day to carve the new dragon's eyes.

HEAD GOBLIN

Solemnly

The dragon hammer will never leave my side again.
Noise of cracking walnuts.

SECOND GOBLIN

But someone is here. Listen.
More sounds of cracking walnuts.

HEAD GOBLIN

Find the human.
They hunt about.
Sniff the air!
They all take a long sniff.

ALL THREE GOBLINS

Aaahhhhh-ha!
They head for the walnut tree and pull Chang-Gil out by
his hair. Head Goblin sits him in the center of the circle.

19

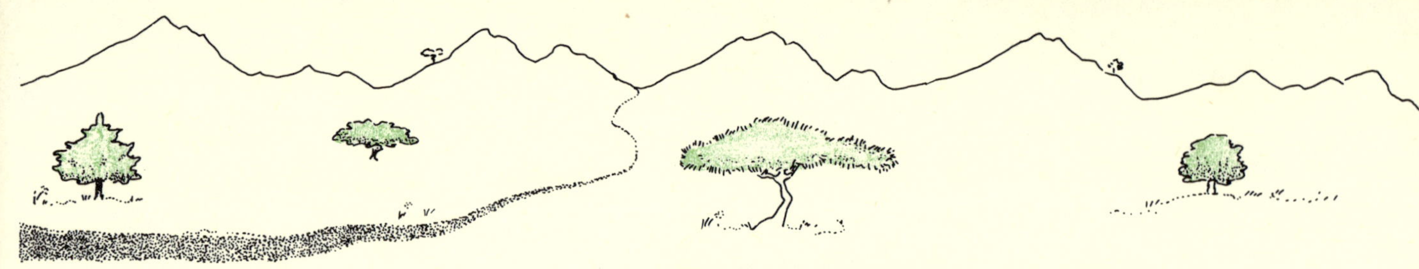

FIRST AND SECOND GOBLINS
Look at him! Look at him! Look at him!

HEAD GOBLIN
Angrily
What is your name?

CHANG-GIL
Frightened
Chang-Gil.

FIRST GOBLIN
Pointing to his face
Interesting . . . a selfish face.

SECOND GOBLIN
Pointing to his feet
Too bad . . . lazy feet.

HEAD GOBLIN
What shall we do with Chang-Gil?

FIRST GOBLIN
HANG HIM!

SECOND GOBLIN
Quickly
NO! He's only a little boy. Punish him instead.

HEAD GOBLIN
Well, what punishment then?
The Goblins walk in a circle around Chang-Gil, then stop.

FIRST GOBLIN
I know this boy. Too selfish to chop wood for his parents.

They walk around again, then stop.

SECOND GOBLIN
I know this boy. Too lazy to make his own kite for the
kite-flying contest.
They walk again, then stop again.

HEAD GOBLIN
I know this boy. While others work, he sleeps.

FIRST GOBLIN
I know this boy. While others work, he eats.

HEAD GOBLIN
Let's stretch his tongue! Thirty feet for selfishness!

FIRST GOBLIN
Forty feet for laziness!

HEAD GOBLIN
Have you anything to say for yourself, Chang-Gil?

CHANG-GIL
Very frightened
Well . . . umm . . . uh . . .

SECOND GOBLIN
Whispers encouragingly
Tell them they're wrong, Chang-Gil. Tell them you do chop wood.
Looking at the axe
I can see he takes good care of his axe.
Puzzled by the strange way Chang-Gil is clutching it
But why are you holding it so strangely?

FIRST GOBLIN
Because he never used an axe in his life. That's why. He stole
this axe.

CHANG-GIL
No, I didn't. I didn't steal the axe. I borrowed it. I'll bring it
back tomorrow.

FIRST GOBLIN
Thirty feet for borrowing without asking.
HEAD GOBLIN
Adding it up
Thirty . . . forty . . . thirty . . . one hundred feet in all!

*The Goblins start moving in a circle around Chang-Gil.
Chang-Gil covers his mouth. The Head Goblin swings,
bends, and pounds the earth with his hammer.*
Tudurag-tag-tag.

FIRST AND SECOND GOBLINS
Tudurag-tag-tag.

HEAD GOBLIN
Tongue grow.

FIRST AND SECOND GOBLINS
Tongue grow.

HEAD GOBLIN
One hundred feet before you stop.

FIRST AND SECOND GOBLINS
One hundred feet before you stop.

HEAD GOBLIN
Tudurag-tag-tag.

FIRST AND SECOND GOBLINS
Tudurag-tag-tag.
*The Goblins make a tight circle around Chang-Gil, and his
tongue begins to unroll. It appears that the tongue is
pushed out in spite of Chang-Gil's struggle. As the Goblins
pull, the enchanted tongue grows longer and longer.*

ALL THREE GOBLINS
Look at him now! Look at him now!
Suddenly the circle breaks.

FIRST GOBLIN
Look out! Here comes Chang-Gil's tongue!

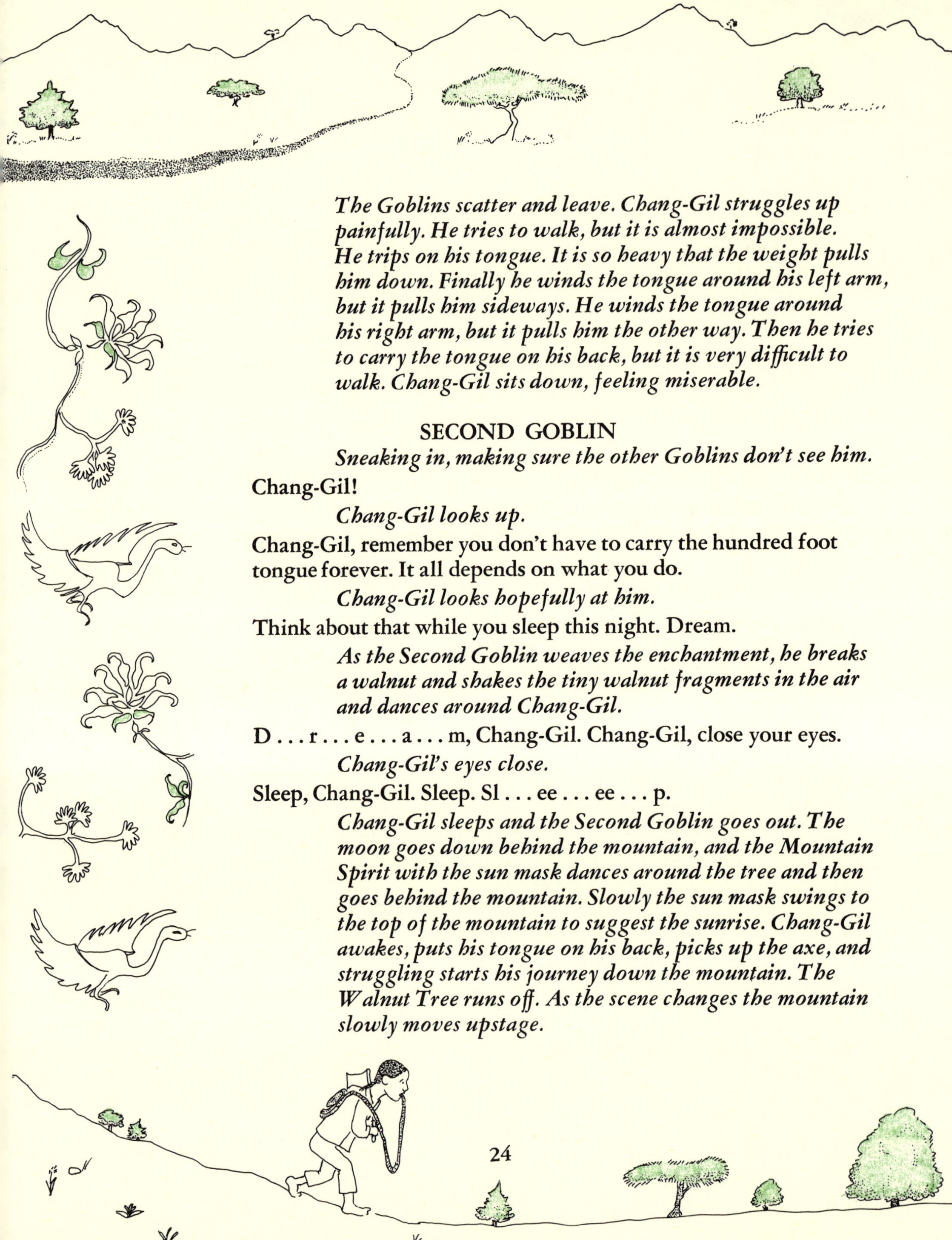

The Goblins scatter and leave. Chang-Gil struggles up
painfully. He tries to walk, but it is almost impossible.
He trips on his tongue. It is so heavy that the weight pulls
him down. Finally he winds the tongue around his left arm,
but it pulls him sideways. He winds the tongue around
his right arm, but it pulls him the other way. Then he tries
to carry the tongue on his back, but it is very difficult to
walk. Chang-Gil sits down, feeling miserable.

SECOND GOBLIN
Sneaking in, making sure the other Goblins don't see him.
Chang-Gil!
Chang-Gil looks up.
Chang-Gil, remember you don't have to carry the hundred foot
tongue forever. It all depends on what you do.
Chang-Gil looks hopefully at him.
Think about that while you sleep this night. Dream.
As the Second Goblin weaves the enchantment, he breaks
a walnut and shakes the tiny walnut fragments in the air
and dances around Chang-Gil.
D . . . r . . . e . . . a . . . m, Chang-Gil. Chang-Gil, close your eyes.
Chang-Gil's eyes close.
Sleep, Chang-Gil. Sleep. Sl . . . ee . . . ee . . . p.
Chang-Gil sleeps and the Second Goblin goes out. The
moon goes down behind the mountain, and the Mountain
Spirit with the sun mask dances around the tree and then
goes behind the mountain. Slowly the sun mask swings to
the top of the mountain to suggest the sunrise. Chang-Gil
awakes, puts his tongue on his back, picks up the axe, and
struggling starts his journey down the mountain. The
Walnut Tree runs off. As the scene changes the mountain
slowly moves upstage.

SCENE FOUR

*A river bank not far from Bang-Su's
home. Chang-Gil enters. He is very,
very tired. He sinks wearily in the corner.
Mother runs on, anxiously peering
towards the river.*

MOTHER

Oh, no! The bridge is cracking! That terrible storm last night.
Oh, if only Bang-Su had his hammer with him—
>   *Screams*
HELP! Come quick!

FIRST VILLAGER

What's wrong?

MOTHER
>   *Still peering out.*
Oh, no! There it goes.

FIRST VILLAGER

What is it?

MOTHER

The bridge. It split in half. Look!

FIRST VILLAGER

What are we going to do?

MOTHER

I was just going down to meet Bang-Su—how will they ever
get home?

Chang-Gil tries to speak, but can't. He tugs at the First Villager to say, "I can help." Without even looking at him, the Villager brushes him aside.

FIRST VILLAGER

Don't bother me, Chang-Gil. You're in the way.
Running back and forth, calling offstage
Help! HELP!

MOTHER

Running back and forth
The bridge is down!
Chang-Gil runs between them trying to get their attention, but he is slowed down by the weight of his tongue. He pantomimes that they should pull his tongue out, but wherever he moves, they are in a different place and do not see him.
Hurry!

FIRST VILLAGER

The bridge to the mountain fell down!
Finally with a tremendous effort Chang-Gil is able to throw his tongue out, but the weight of it forces him to the ground. The Mother and First Villager finally understand and help unroll the tongue so that it stretches across the stage toward the mountain. After a moment of anxious waiting, Bang-Su crosses the tongue bridge.

BANG-SU

With relief
We thought we wouldn't see the village again for a week. All of a sudden—how did you repair the bridge so fast?

Mother points to Chang-Gil's tongue. Bang-Su runs to the end of it and sees Chang-Gil.

Oh, Chang-Gil.

Sympathetically.

You must be tired and hungry.

MOTHER

And thirsty.

Chang-Gil nods, appreciating a friendly word, and returns Bang-Su's axe.

Thank you, Chang-Gil. Wait, the other villagers are coming now. I'll be right back.

Bang-Su and Mother go out as the other villagers cross the tongue bridge.

SECOND VILLAGER

What kind of bridge is this?

THIRD VILLAGER

Tapping tongue

It isn't wood.

SECOND VILLAGER

Or stone.

FIRST VILLAGER

Waiting for them to discover what it is

But it brought you home!

The Second and Third Villagers investigate the tongue further.

SECOND VILLAGER

No, it certainly isn't silk.

THIRD VILLAGER
It's definitely not clay.

BANG-SU
Running on with his dragon hammer
But one word makes it go away!
He swings, bends, and pounds the earth.
Tudurag-tag-tag. Tudurag-tag-tag. Tongue, shrink.
The Villagers crowd around Chang-Gil, hiding him. When he stands up, the enchanted tongue is gone. He is very stiff.

CHANG-GIL
Bowing painfully.
Komawaw! Thank you.

MOTHER
Entering with a bowl of water.
Here's some water for your tired tongue.
Chang-Gil drinks it carefully.

FIRST AND SECOND VILLAGERS
Komawaw!

SECOND VILLAGER
We would have been there for days without your help.

CHANG-GIL
And now let's repair that bridge before any more travellers try to cross. We'd better hurry.

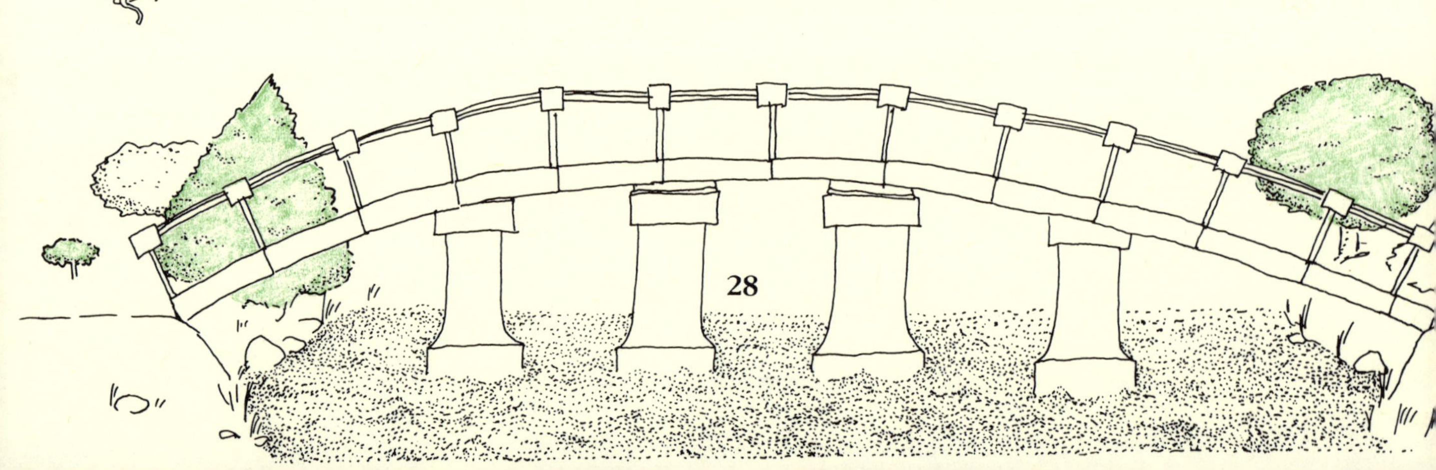

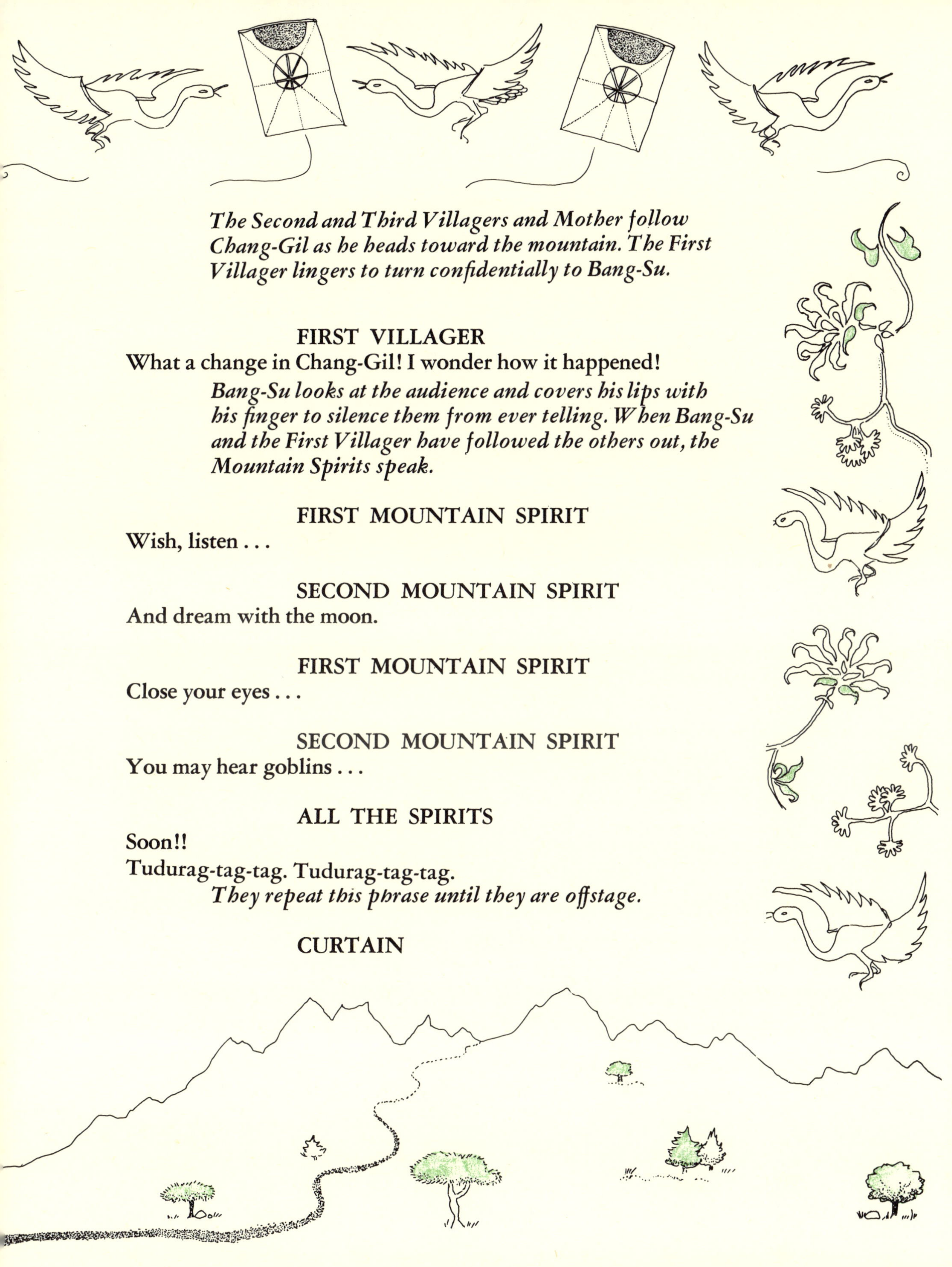

*The Second and Third Villagers and Mother follow
Chang-Gil as he heads toward the mountain. The First
Villager lingers to turn confidentially to Bang-Su.*

FIRST VILLAGER

What a change in Chang-Gil! I wonder how it happened!
*Bang-Su looks at the audience and covers his lips with
his finger to silence them from ever telling. When Bang-Su
and the First Villager have followed the others out, the
Mountain Spirits speak.*

FIRST MOUNTAIN SPIRIT

Wish, listen . . .

SECOND MOUNTAIN SPIRIT

And dream with the moon.

FIRST MOUNTAIN SPIRIT

Close your eyes . . .

SECOND MOUNTAIN SPIRIT

You may hear goblins . . .

ALL THE SPIRITS

Soon!!
Tudurag-tag-tag. Tudurag-tag-tag.
They repeat this phrase until they are offstage.

CURTAIN

PRODUCTION NOTES

"THE DRAGON HAMMER"

COSTUMES:

    2 traditional Korean boys' pants and jackets
    1 traditional Korean woman's blouse and long skirt
    3 traditional costumes for the villagers
    1 walnut tree costume
    3 goblin masks or headdresses

PROPERTIES:

Most of the properties are imagined, and pantomimed when they are used.
    1 small wooden hammer decorated with a dragon
    1 sun mask carried on a long pole
    1 moon carried on a long pole
    Walnuts
    Boots
    A Korean kite
    1 long tongue made of any pink-red material that will roll easily
      (Crepe paper is inexpensive)
    A bowl of water

SETTINGS:

    1 painted cloth that represents a mountain
    1 set piece that represents Bang-Su's mud hut with thatched roof
    1 large storage jar

LIGHTING:

    If performed indoors, the stage should darken when it is night.

SOUND:

    A favorite Korean folk song, such as "Ari-Rang," could introduce and end the play.

The Tale of Oniroku

Cast of Characters

Taro, the carpenter

Oniroku, the ogre

Ohana, a village woman

Aya, a village woman

Tadashi, an elderly man, fond of food

Mansaku, a young village man

Three young ogres

Three actors who represent the mountain and the trees

Settings

By the bend in the river on the outskirts of a Japanese village, and in an enchanted wood.

SCENE ONE

*It is early morning in autumn by the river bank.
OHANA and AYA are on their way to market with
baskets of cabbages and apples. TADASHI is on his way
to visit his granddaughter. MANSAKU is on his way to
buy more oakwood, so that he can finish building his
new home. All are talking about their day's plans as
they enter.*

OHANA
Sets her baskets down

Not again! The bridge is down. That's the fourth time in
two moons.

Others enter

AYA

How can I go to market?

TADASHI

How can I got to visit my granddaughter?
Sits unhappily

I'll be late . . . and she prepared tea cakes especially. She makes
the most delicious rice cakes. No one on this side of the river
knows how.

MANSAKU

Something must be done! But since summer none of our men
have been able to build a bridge strong enough.

32

OHANA

It's as though the river doesn't want us to get across.

AYA

What good are my cabbages if I can't get to market?
They'll just spoil if I don't sell them.

TADASHI

Solemnly

It's just as though there were an ancient river ogre guarding
the water.

MANSAKU

Oh, Tadashi! I'm sure there's a simple explanation. Too much rain
or wind, but not river ogres.

OHANA

I remember my ancestors talked about them, Tadashi, but that
was long ago.

TADASHI

Not so long ago. The last one was a hundred years ago, and some
say they come every hundred years.

MANSAKU

You're being silly, all of you. All we need is a carpenter.
Sees TARO
And there's one from the next village.
Calls
Taro, come here. We need your help.

OHANA

Some say there's magic in the hammer Taro uses.

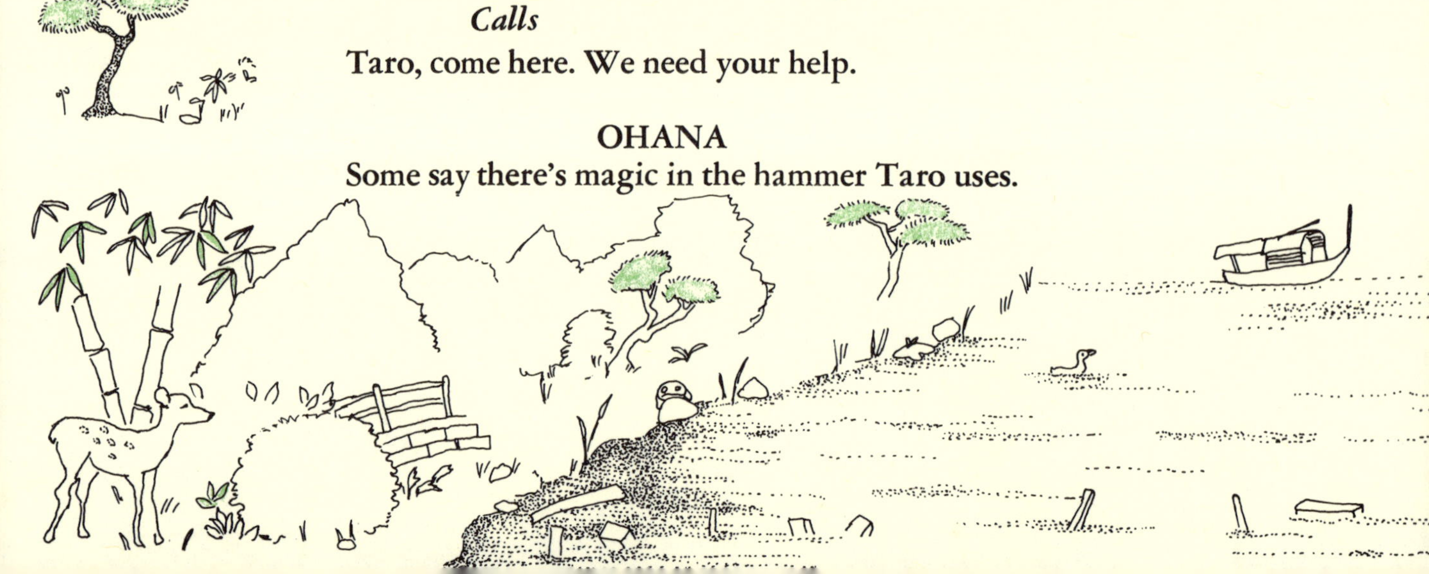

AYA

I've heard that whatever he builds lasts forever.

MANSAKU

Then he's just the one to ask.

TARO
> *Enters. All bow low in greeting*

Good morning to you all.
> *As he looks up he sees the broken bridge*

What! Your bridge has collapsed again! My friends, why fight this angry river? Why don't you just come to live in our village? We will make room.

OHANA

Thank you. But we don't want to move to another village.

MANSAKU

I've just built a new home of solid oak wood. In fact I was just on my way across the river to buy the last load of wood I'd need.

OHANA

And we have apples . . . just ripening.

AYA

And cabbages . . . ready to sell.

MANSAKU

But what we do want is a bridge, Taro. Can you build us one that will last?

TADASHI
> *Stubbornly*

The more I think about it, the more I think there's a river ogre

35

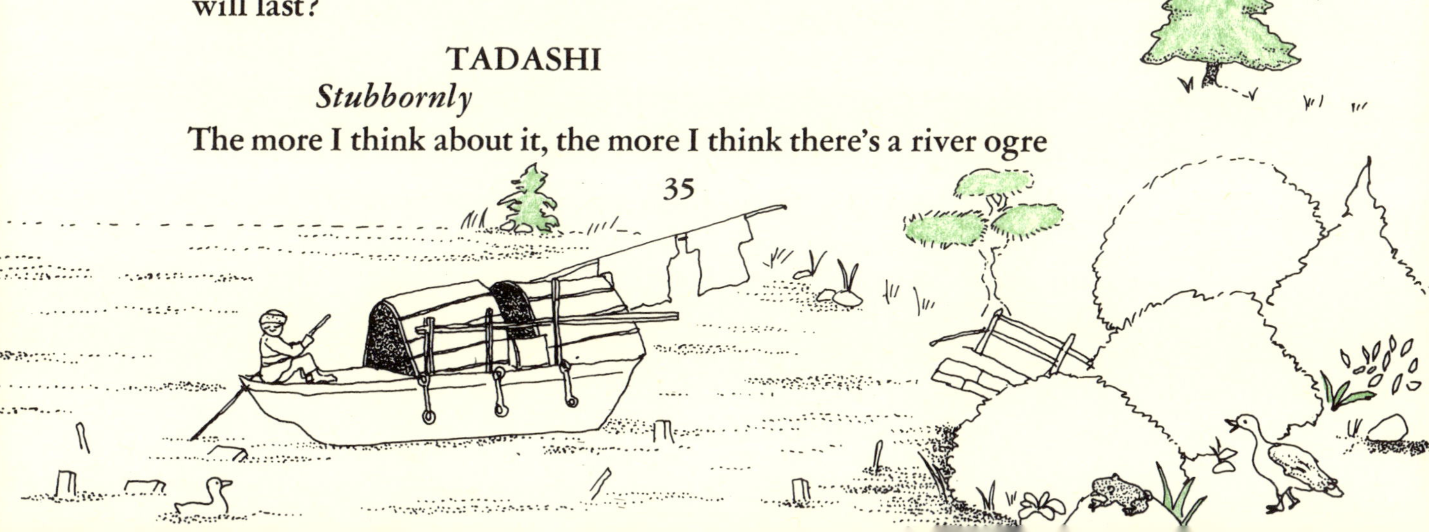

below. A river ogre who doesn't want us here . . . or who wants something from us. A new bridge won't do any good. It will just get broken like the others.

TARO

My great-grandmother spoke about river ogres too, but Tadashi, that was long ago! All she said was that they had terrible eyes and a terrible memory. Nothing about breaking bridges. She said it was easy to fool them if you were clever, and you see, she was right. They've all been killed off long ago.

TADASHI

Long ago? Perhaps. But no bridge we have built since summer has lasted one full moon. Why is that? The oak wood is the same.

TARO

That's simple. You've had storms and floods. The bridges have not been strong enough to stand against the wind and water.

MANSAKU

Taro, you are the best carpenter we know. You're the only one who can build a bridge strong enough to withstand heavy winds and rising waters. Will you build our bridge?

TARO

Let me examine what's left of the bridge and the swiftness of the current. I will build you the strongest bridge I can. But leave me now to begin my work.
>   *Villagers go out thanking him*
But a bridge that will last forever is impossible. No man can do that.
>   *Looks at the rapid current where the bridge had been*
But it is strange. Why have they all broken since summer?

Examines broken piece of wood
This is our best wood. It should not snap in the wind.
*There is a loud splashing noise and TARO moves back
frightened. OGRE appears, shields his eyes from sunlight.*

OGRE
Isn't anyone going to ask me what I think?

TARO
Terrified
Who are you?

OGRE
Oh, you'll find out. But first answer me. Who are you?

TARO
Bravely
Taro the carpenter. The villagers want me to build a bridge here
. . . over the river.

OGRE
Well you can't. I won't let you. I rule this river. Why do you think
I knocked all the others down? If anyone were going to build a
bridge, I would. The river ogre is the only one who knows the
secret of the river's speed.

TARO
To himself
River ogre! So that's why.

37

OGRE

Your human bridges won't last more than a moon. No! The
answer is no. No bridge . . .

> *Slyly, pauses, ready to bargain*

unless . . .

TARO

Oh yes! My great-grandmother said, "You can always bargain with
a river ogre."

> *Making an offer*

When the villagers pay me, I'll give you half.

OGRE

Half! Half indeed! That's little enough. Besides, what would I do
with your money? There's nothing to buy down here.

TARO

What then? I have very little to offer. Carpenters are not rich.
They are not emperors.

> *OGRE studies him*

I haven't any jewels, if that's what you're looking for.
But l do have a fine sword.

> *Flourishes it*

OGRE

> *Not interested*

It would rust down here.

> *Slowly*

What I want is something small, something you won't even need
once the bridge is done.

TARO

Gladly, river ogre. What is it?

OGRE

Come closer, and I will tell you.

TARO does

OGRE

Closer . . .

TARO takes another step

Closer!

TARO takes one more step

I want to see as well as humans do. What I want is . . .

OGRE leaps up

YOUR EYES!

TARO

Stunned

My eyes! Surely you can not be so cruel that you would stop me from working. A carpenter's eyes are more important than his hammer and nails.

OGRE

If you do not promise me, I will not build your bridge.

Fiercely

And if I do not build it for you, no one else will . . . EVER.

Slyly

On the other hand, Taro, if I do build it your people can cross the river forever in safety. The bridge will never collapse. Do you want to be remembered only as a selfish man? After all, what is a small item like two eyes compared with the safety and happiness of the village?

TARO stands there frightened trying to make a decision

Quickly, quickly, Taro. I haven't all day.

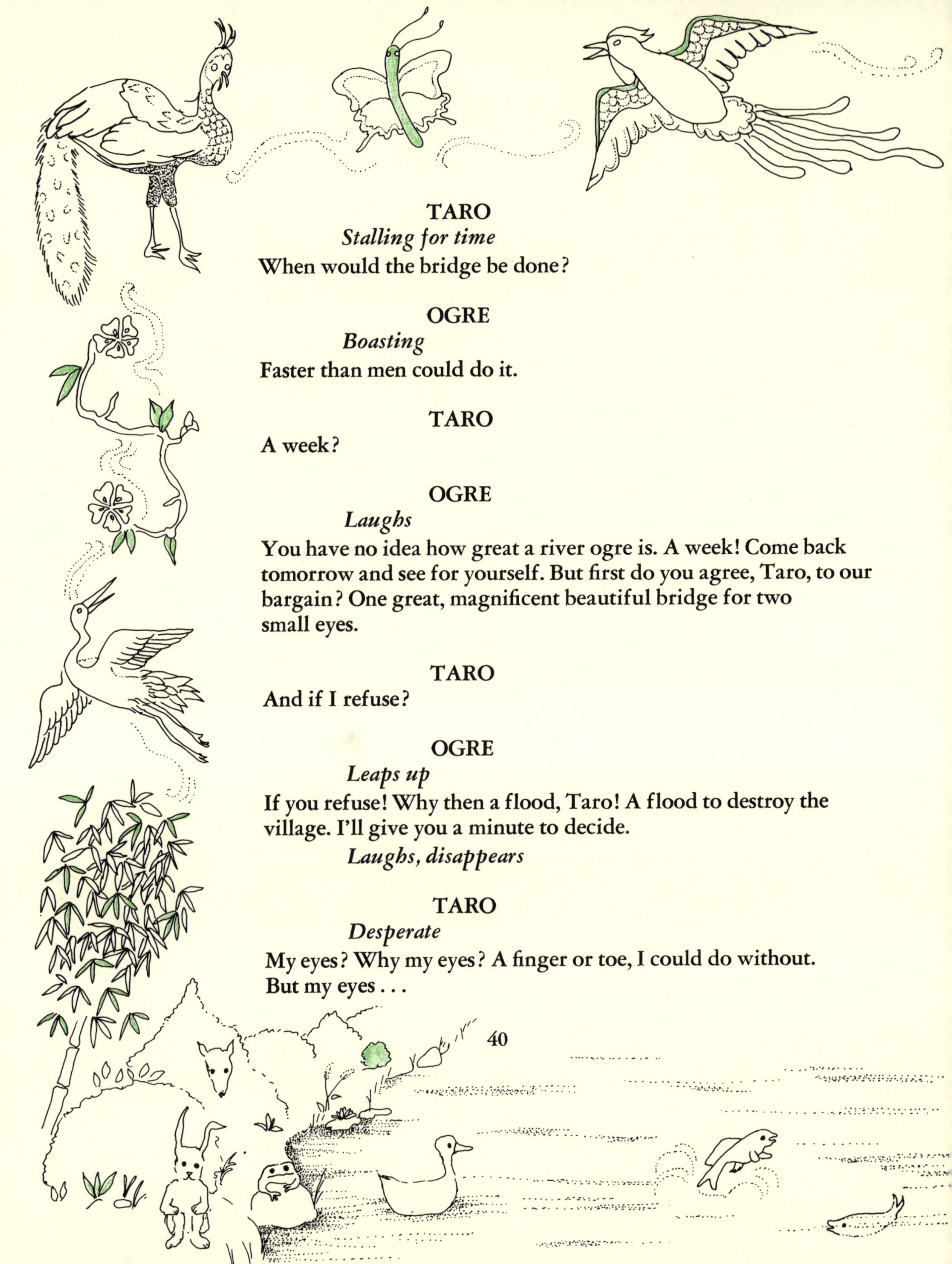

TARO
Stalling for time
When would the bridge be done?

OGRE
Boasting
Faster than men could do it.

TARO
A week?

OGRE
Laughs
You have no idea how great a river ogre is. A week! Come back
tomorrow and see for yourself. But first do you agree, Taro, to our
bargain? One great, magnificent beautiful bridge for two
small eyes.

TARO
And if I refuse?

OGRE
Leaps up
If you refuse! Why then a flood, Taro! A flood to destroy the
village. I'll give you a minute to decide.
Laughs, disappears

TARO
Desperate
My eyes? Why my eyes? A finger or toe, I could do without.
But my eyes . . .

40

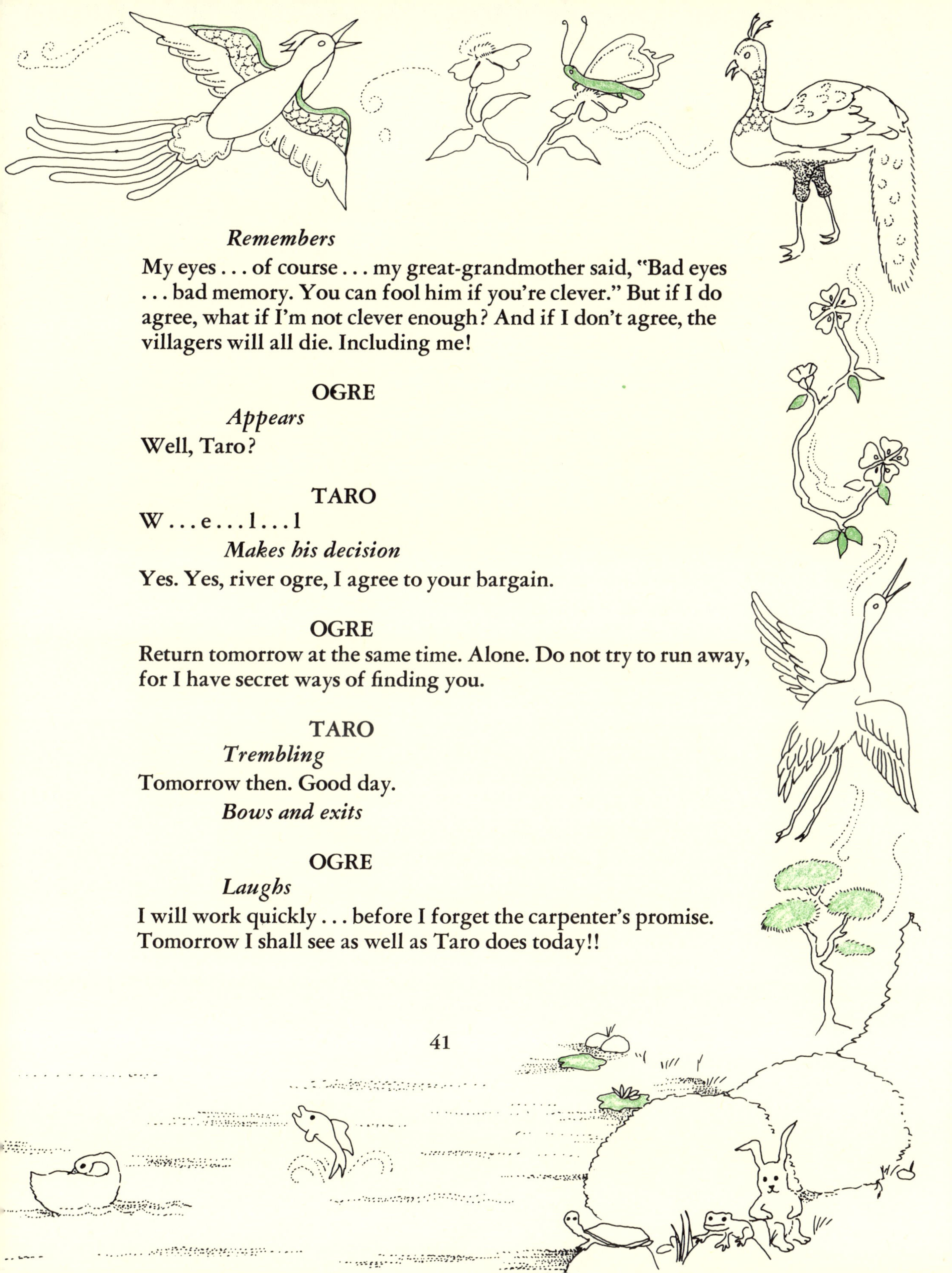

Remembers

My eyes . . . of course . . . my great-grandmother said, "Bad eyes
. . . bad memory. You can fool him if you're clever." But if I do
agree, what if I'm not clever enough? And if I don't agree, the
villagers will all die. Including me!

OGRE

Appears

Well, Taro?

TARO

W . . . e . . . l . . . l

Makes his decision

Yes. Yes, river ogre, I agree to your bargain.

OGRE

Return tomorrow at the same time. Alone. Do not try to run away,
for I have secret ways of finding you.

TARO

Trembling

Tomorrow then. Good day.

Bows and exits

OGRE

Laughs

I will work quickly . . . before I forget the carpenter's promise.
Tomorrow I shall see as well as Taro does today!!

Laughs. The stage darkens. There is the sound of ancient
Japanese music, as the OGRE dances his way across the
stage, letting the arched bridge unfold before our eyes.
He surveys his work, stretches, yawns and goes to sleep.
Slowly the lights come up and TARO enters. He looks in
the direction of the river. He rubs his eyes.

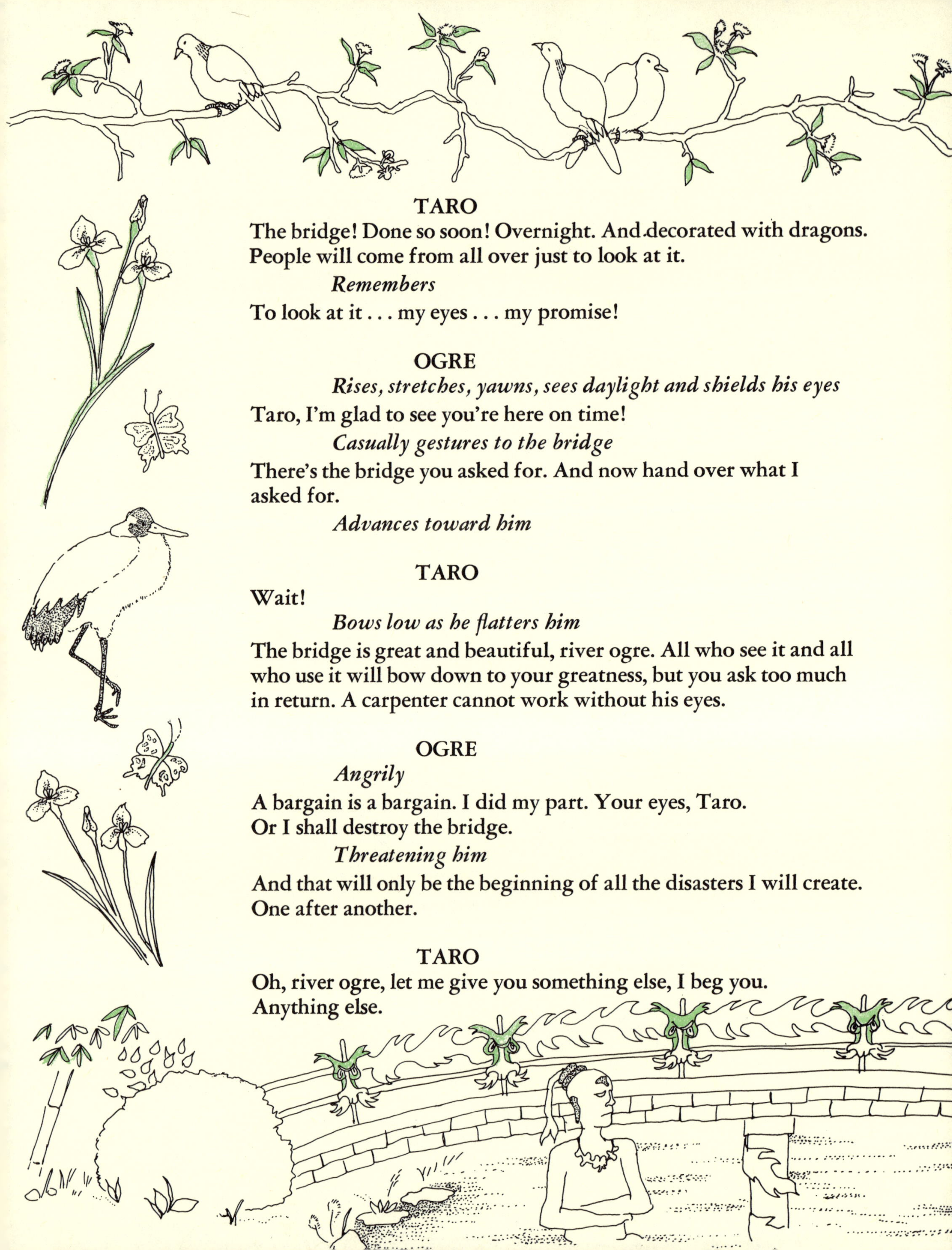

TARO

The bridge! Done so soon! Overnight. And decorated with dragons.
People will come from all over just to look at it.

> *Remembers*

To look at it . . . my eyes . . . my promise!

OGRE

> *Rises, stretches, yawns, sees daylight and shields his eyes*

Taro, I'm glad to see you're here on time!

> *Casually gestures to the bridge*

There's the bridge you asked for. And now hand over what I
asked for.

> *Advances toward him*

TARO

Wait!

> *Bows low as he flatters him*

The bridge is great and beautiful, river ogre. All who see it and all
who use it will bow down to your greatness, but you ask too much
in return. A carpenter cannot work without his eyes.

OGRE

> *Angrily*

A bargain is a bargain. I did my part. Your eyes, Taro.
Or I shall destroy the bridge.

> *Threatening him*

And that will only be the beginning of all the disasters I will create.
One after another.

TARO

Oh, river ogre, let me give you something else, I beg you.
Anything else.

OGRE

No. You humans are all alike. All I want is something you won't
even need a hundred years from now, but something that I could
use for a thousand. Not even a thank you for my work. That bridge
was not easy to build in one night.

Hurt

You didn't even admire the dragons.

TARO

Looks at them to appease ogre

They are very frightening.

OGRE

Magnificent you mean! Now, hand over your eyes.

TARO

Pleading

River ogre, you have kept your part of the bargain, and if you
would wait a mere fifty years, I'll be glad to give you my eyes then.
I'm only asking for time. Time to admire your bridge. To study and
learn from this great masterpiece for there is none other like it in
the land. Surely fifty years is little enough time to request to keep
my eyes when you will have them for a thousand.

OGRE

Affected by the flattery, he softens a little

So it's time you want now. Very well, since you're only a mortal,
I'll be glad to give you some time.

TARO

Jumps up, overjoyed

Oh, thank you river ogre. Thank you!!

45

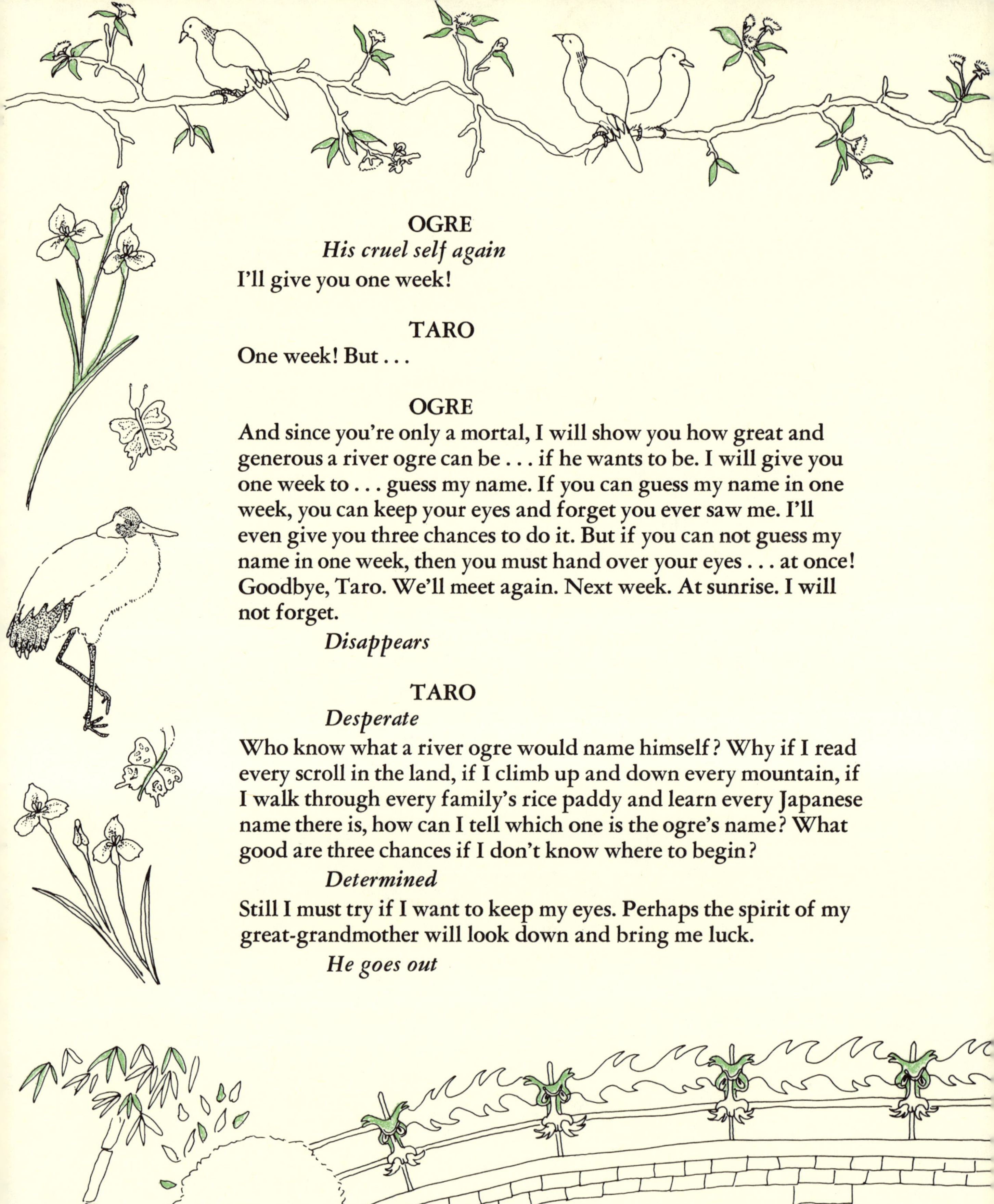

OGRE

His cruel self again

I'll give you one week!

TARO

One week! But . . .

OGRE

And since you're only a mortal, I will show you how great and generous a river ogre can be . . . if he wants to be. I will give you one week to . . . guess my name. If you can guess my name in one week, you can keep your eyes and forget you ever saw me. I'll even give you three chances to do it. But if you can not guess my name in one week, then you must hand over your eyes . . . at once! Goodbye, Taro. We'll meet again. Next week. At sunrise. I will not forget.

Disappears

TARO

Desperate

Who know what a river ogre would name himself? Why if I read every scroll in the land, if I climb up and down every mountain, if I walk through every family's rice paddy and learn every Japanese name there is, how can I tell which one is the ogre's name? What good are three chances if I don't know where to begin?

Determined

Still I must try if I want to keep my eyes. Perhaps the spirit of my great-grandmother will look down and bring me luck.

He goes out

SCENE TWO

This scene is done using an actor as the mountain. During the change from Scene One to Scene Two the actor, covered in a cloth painted with mountain colors, capped with a white peak of snow, crouches on the stage. By the actor's rising movement under the cloth, the "mountain" seems to rise and loom before Taro. As Taro stands in place and pretends to climb, the "Mountain" rises very slowly.

Taro walks on wearily, covered with dust and grime.

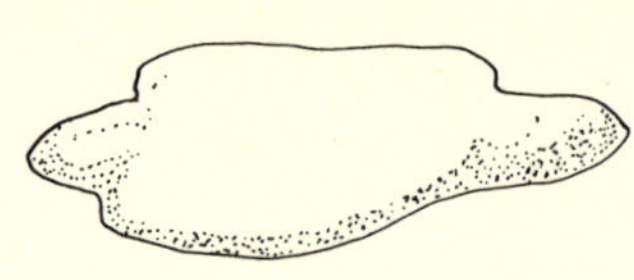
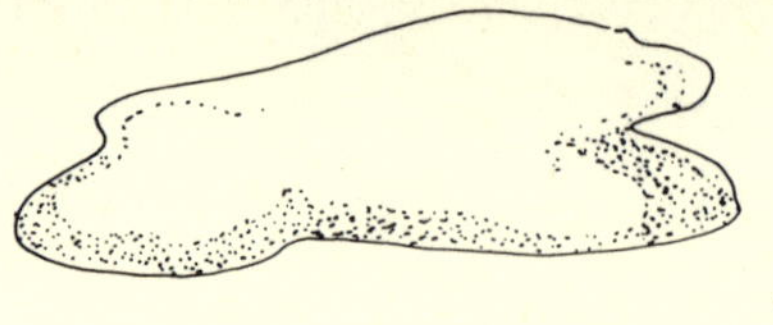

TARO

Nearly a week. I still don't know the ogre's name . . . and now there is the mountain to cross.

Bows low

Oh, great and mighty mountain, if ever you helped travellers find good fortune, help me now. Help the villagers keep their new bridge to cross the river. Help me to keep my old eyes to see my work.

He gazes around him

Why I can see the ocean from here. How it shines in the morning sunlight! The country looks so beautiful . . . so peaceful . . .

Looks sharply at one area

all except that dark part. It looks like . . .

Searches his memory

It looks like the description that my great-grandmother gave of the enchanted forest. So dark . . . so evil . . . the land home of the river ogre! Maybe, that's where I'll find out his name.

Bows low

Oh, mountain, direct my feet the quickest way!

Taro comes down the mountain the same way he climbed it, except that he seems to move with greater speed and sureness. When he reaches the bottom, the mountain crumples. He turns toward the wood. The stage darkens and there are eerie forest noises. The "trees" are actors who spread their arms like branches. Their movements are sinister as though they wished to frighten TARO away.

Offstage there is the sound of evil laughter. TARO stops. He crouches behind a tree, staying close to the ground,

48

*and watches. THREE SMALL OGRES come on carrying
a black pot and spoon. They are followed by the RIVER
OGRE.*

OGRE
Come! Come! My supper. I'm hungry.

FIRST SMALL OGRE
When will the carpenter come?

SECOND SMALL OGRE
I want to see him. I never saw a human.

THIRD SMALL OGRE
I hope his eyes are really better than mine. Then I can leave this
dark forest and see what the sun looks like.

FIRST
Well, you'll never find out. Because those eyes are for me.
I'm the oldest.

SECOND
No, me!
> *Furious*

THIRD
No, me! It was my idea.

OGRE
> *Growling*

Where's my supper?

*THREE SMALL OGRES dance around the black pot,
stirring and chanting*

SMALL OGRES

Tomorrow, tomorrow we'll see the sun
Tomorrow, tomorrow, Taro's week is done!

> *At the first mention of his name TARO pays strict
> attention. He raises his head slightly, but makes sure
> that the ogres don't see him.*

SMALL OGRES

They mimic people with disdain

"River ogre. River Ogre." That's all those humans can say. But his
real name, ONIROKU, only we can say!!

OGRE

QUIET! What if someone heard you? Let's have some supper and
go to sleep. Tomorrow is an important day!

> *They eat noisly, grabbing the spoon from one another,
> leaving the ogre to lick the pot. The THREE SMALL
> OGRES curl up to go to sleep. The OGRE curls up nearby*

SMALL OGRES

Chanting happily and rocking in their sleep

My eyes! My eyes! My eyes!

OGRE

Growls

My eyes!

51

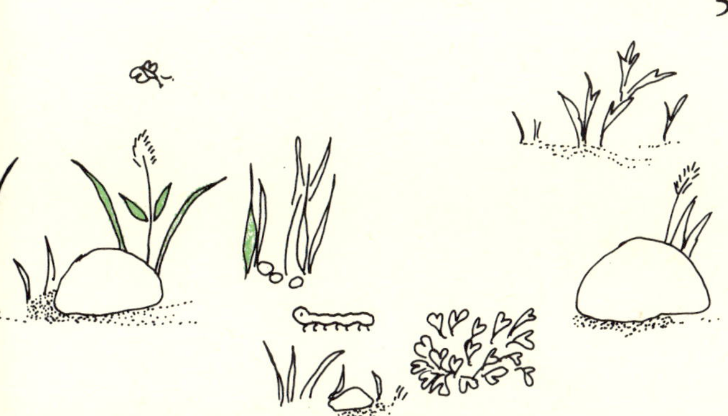

SMALL OGRES

Repeat

My eyes! My eyes! My eyes!

Light comes up on the carpenter

TARO

Firmly

MY EYES!!!

TARO goes back the same way he came, past the trees and over the mountain. This time he is joyful. At the bottom of the mountain, he bows low.

Thank you, mighty mountain. And now to the riverbank!

52

SCENE THREE

The river bank we saw in Scene One, new bridge added.
It is early morning and Taro enters, running

TARO

Finally! The river bank. Good, the bridge is still here, and the sun
is just rising by the mountain top. I'm in time.

OGRE

Appears

Well, carpenter, I have no time to waste. Take your last look
around, then give me your eyes.

TARO

Remember your promise.

OGRE

Promise? Oh yes. Well, go ahead. Guess my name, if you can.

TARO

Teasing him

I searched and searched. Near the mountains, I met someone
who said your name was . . . DAISAKU.

OGRE

Laughs
WRONG!!

53

TARO
And then I travelled further and further, and a farmer said it
had to be . . . SHINROKU.

OGRE
Laughs
Wrong again! Only one more chance, carpenter. Be prepared
to lose your eyes.

TARO
Ignores him
And then as I travelled further, I came to a strange wood . . .

OGRE
Smile disappears, asks sharply
What wood?

TARO
And *there* I saw three small ogres and one large ogre, and
there I heard your name . . . ONIROKU!!!

OGRE
Furious, growls
If my eyes had been better, I'd have seen you! Well, this time,
mortal, you have won. But next time, I'll win.

TARO
Making sure
Remember, Oniroku, you said if I guessed your name correctly,
that I could keep my eyes.

OGRE
Well, keep them, then. A river ogre keeps his word. But in return,
Taro, you must forget you ever saw me or all of this work will
be undone.
    Points to the bridge, casts a spell
For the story of this bridge can never be told,
Until we are both older than old.
    TARO falls to the ground. He sleeps.
Goodbye. I shall return in a hundred years.
    OGRE disappears

TARO
    Wakes up. He has forgotten what happened.
Such a strange dream.
    Trying to remember it
I can't . . . remember . . . it . . . something about . .
    Looks around
Did I sleep here all night?
    VILLAGERS rush on

55

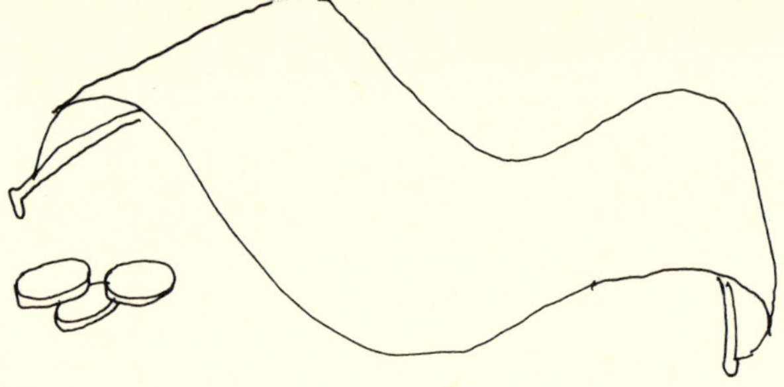

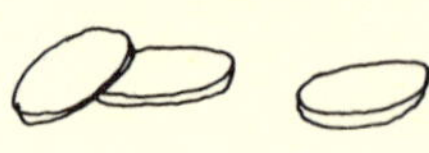

TADASHI
Where have you been?

AYA
Taro, the Emperor himself has heard of your bridge. And he has sent fine jade in your honor.

OHANA
Look at the lacquered box he sent it in. And the box has a chrysanthemum on it too—the Imperial Crest! Now everyone will know of your honor.

MANSAKU
In the name of the Emperor and in the name of our village, accept our humble thanks and payment.
 Ceremoniously hands him box, and bag of coins.
 Both men bow.

TADASHI
 Talking about bridge, excitedly
The bridge is not only strong . . .

56

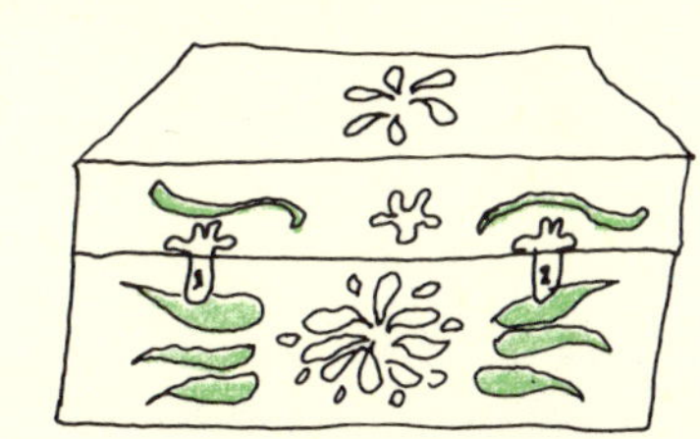
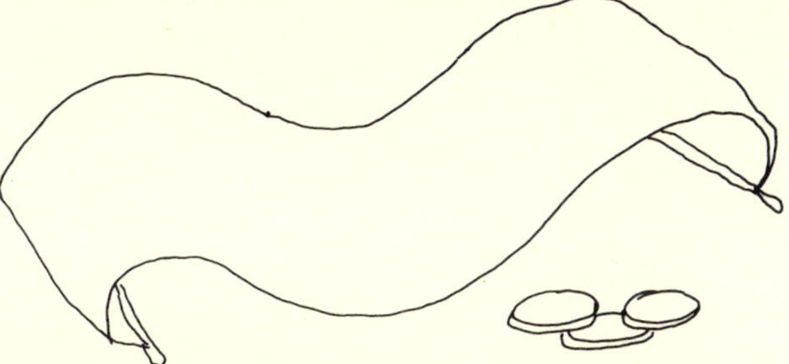

AYA
Interrupting
It's beautiful too. My feet feel light whenever I cross it.

MANSAKU
There is no other bridge like it.

TARO
Confused
It is a mystery I, myself, do not understand.

OHANA
Since the dragon bridge, I've sold all my vegetables every day!

MANSAKU
My friends, let us make today a holiday in our village.
We'll call it . . . "The Great Carpenter's Day"!

OTHERS
Ah, yes. Yes. What a good idea!

TARO
No, my friends, not in honor of me. In honor of the dragon bridge.
Now that you can cross the river.

TADASHI

Excited

And now that we can *all* cross the river, come with me and taste
the finest rice cakes from here to the Emperor's Palace!

*They go out laughing. TARO is the center of attention.
There is the faint sound of Japanese music, the same
sound we heard when the bridge was first built.*

THE END

PRODUCTION NOTES
"THE TALE OF ONIKORU"

COSTUMES:
6 appropriate Japanese costumes
4 grotesque ogre costumes
1 cloth for mountain
2 tree costumes

PROPERTIES:
1 sword
1 black pot and spoon
1 lacquered box and bag of money

SETTINGS:
You may want to use a ground row (a long, low piece of scenery) which represents the river bank with rocks, tall grasses, etc.

1 ground row, which represents the river with a few waves for Scenes One and Three.

1 paper bridge. The bridge the Ogre puts up should be arched in the tradition of Japanese bridges and hung between the rock and the wave. It should be decorated with dragons and impressive to look at.

LIGHTING:
Daylight effects except in Scene One when the Ogre builds the bridge and in Scene Two in the woods. When the Ogre builds the bridge, the stage should darken. In the wood there should be an eerie lighting effect.

SOUND:
Splashing water
Ancient Japanese music

A NOTE FOR
PARENTS AND TEACHERS

The Dragon Hammer and *The Tale of Oniroku* are written to introduce children to the pleasures—and the typographic conventions—of reading plays. But they are also ideal vehicles for young performers to produce.

Both plays have been very successfully used in third to fifth grade classrooms, with the teacher involving the whole class in study of the cultures and folklore involved, art projects, improvisations of the scenes, and a final presentation of the play, either just for the pleasure of the group, or sometimes sharing with parents and another class.

The plays also lend themselves to production outside the school setting—as a project for a club, the culminating activity for a summer camp program, a fund-raiser for a neighborhood "gang," or simply backyard fun.

An informal children's production of a play poses a dilemma not unlike playground athletics. How much adult supervision is required or desired? Too little, and the whole project may fall apart. Too much, and it becomes the adult's project, not the child's.

Generally speaking, children love putting on plays, but carrying through a production calls for organizational skills and experience in handling people that children rarely acquire before their teens. So it's important for an adult to stand by with generous background support when a child wants to put on a play, and oversee the direction.

When it comes to props, costumes, scenery, programs, and ticket sales, on the other hand, I've found many young people willing and able to take responsibility for planning and carrying through the whole job. All you may need to do is supply generous quantities of paper, cardboard, marking-pens and paint, scissors, strong tape and old sheets.

The direction you provide does not require specialized talent or training, but it does call for a certain amount of time, energy, planning and organization. Having some experience in the theatre is an asset, but even more is a sense of enjoying children's creative endeavors.

To discover some guidelines for a typical informal production, I enlisted my own two children and seven of their friends and neighbors, ranging in age from six to thirteen, in preparing a performance of *The Dragon Hammer.* The schedule we worked out may be helpful to you.

Timing. We found six or seven rehearsals over a two to three week period worked out well. I've seen plays lose their spontaneity and momentum when they stretched out too long. You also lose momentum if you let more than three or four days go between rehearsals. If a group meets once a week—

like Scouts or Sunday School—schedule several midweek sessions for the duration of the play. I usually planned an hour and a half to two hours per session, sometimes more to allow more time for eating, playing, and artwork.

Casting. At the first meeting we began with about fifteen minutes of theatre games and movement improvisations—the sort of "warm-ups" to be found in a good creative dramatics book. I spent a while working with the full group in unison on actions that would later be incorporated into the play—simple pantomime like becoming a setting sun or eating rice cakes, and more elaborate actions like using magic words to put spells on people or things, first using the children's ideas and then introducing the action from the play. Then I told the story in considerable detail, sometimes stopping for questions like "What do you think Bang-Su did then?" We talked about the characters and what they did, and tried out some of their actions—the Goblin somersaults, Bang-Su chopping wood, Chang-Gil stealing the kite, etc.

By now you should have a good idea of which part is right for which child. The plays lend themselves to flexible casting. Any part can be done by either a boy or a girl. If you have more children than parts, more children can be added to the groups, like goblins or villagers. Younger or shyer children work out well in the non-speaking roles like mountains and trees. You may well want to switch parts around as you go along.

We ended the session by passing out scripts, reading through the play together, and setting up a schedule for the rest of the rehearsals and the performance. Having this schedule in writing, with time, place, transportation arrangements, etc., is a great help to everybody.

Rehearsing. The next time we met we started working intensively on the first scene. We worked slowly, discussing and trying out different ideas for achieving various effects, planning the necessary scenery, deciding which props would be real and which pantomimed. This is a good time for clearing up mispronunciations and working out or changing lines the children have trouble with. Don't be anxious about sticking to the script word for word. One reason I like these plays is that their structures are sturdy and the characters clear-cut, allowing plenty of room for improvisation, elaboration, and individual variation within each scene.

After a scene is "set," go over it two or three times. By then the children will know it well enough to start memorizing the lines or to improvise it without the script.

I had brought a supply of drawing paper and marking pens, and before we started work on the second scene, we took a half hour to make invitations and programs. They all loved doing this—I think it helps them visualize the finished product of their work, and solidifies their commitment to the project. I Xeroxed some of the artwork to use as invitations to be passed out to family and friends, and used the rest for program covers.

Before the next rehearsal I picked up several of the older children for a trip to the library. I had telephoned the librarian, and she had several suggestions for books ready for us, and found a Korean record which we used as our "overture." We made some sketches of thatched houses and kites, and checked out the most useful books. This is not an activity that appeals to everybody, but it's stimulating for the book-oriented, and I noticed at the next rehearsal that everyone was looking through the books we checked out.

As we continued work on scenes Three and Four, we talked about costumes and props, and the children made lists of what they would bring from home for the next rehearsal. We also made the sun and moon masks, and did sketches from the books of the house and the kimchee jar.

The next two rehearsals were spent going through the entire play, adding sound and lighting effects as the children worked them out, and completing work on the scenery. Everybody loved tie-dyeing the mountain (an old sheet) to achieve green and brown banks and a white snow-capped peak.

By the fifth session the children should be working without scripts, with prompting as necessary. We spent most of a Saturday together, working on scenery and practicing difficult spots in the morning, and after lunch going through the whole play twice. You might want to separate this into two sessions. I made a shopping list of makeup and sent it home with an interested mother.

The performance. We assembled an hour and a half before "curtain time" to allow lots of time for makeup. Creating weird Goblin faces and exotic Oriental eyes, with the help of the mother who had shopped for the makeup, was great fun for everybody. I handled sound-effects and prompting, and one of the children did "lighting"—which mainly consisted of switching the dining room lights off and on.

Last-minute jitters and even tears, forgotten lines and wobbly scenery can all be part of the final session. A few theatre games help relax the children before the performance, and a packet of safety pins can repair many disasters, but it helps even more to remember that the point of doing a play with children is not a polished production. You're giving them an opportunity for growth and interaction, a different way of enjoying literature by participating in it, a way of projecting themselves imaginatively into another culture and another self. All these have been well served by the process of developing and performing the play, and that matters more than the perfection of the final product. The teacher/parent/director's success lies in the question, "When can we put on another play?"

Patricia Whitton
Publisher